100

MIND-BLOWING
AI
FACTS

100 Shocking Ways Artificial Intelligence is Changing the World

FELIX GRAYSON

MINDSPARK
PUBLISHING

Published by MindSpark Publishing.
Cover design by MindSpark Publishing.

CONTENTS

BEFORE WE DIVE IN...

Did you know that this is just **one** of many **mind-blowing** books waiting to be discovered?

What if I told you there's a **world of jaw-dropping, unbelievable, and downright bizarre facts** across **sports, science, history, mysteries, and more**—each one packed with stories that will **challenge what you thought you knew?**

EVER WONDERED WHAT IT'S LIKE TO...

- Witness **record-breaking Olympic moments** that defy human limits?

- Explore **real-life conspiracy theories** that sound too wild to be true?

- Discover **unsolved mysteries** that still leave experts baffled?

- Learn about **billionaires, stock market**

crashes, and money secrets?

- Find out how **robots, AI, and space travel are shaping the future?**

- Experience the **most extreme sports, legendary battles, and shocking events?**

This is just the beginning. The **100 Mind-Blowing series** covers it **all.**

WANT TO SEE WHAT'S NEXT?

Go to **FelixGrayson.com** and explore the **growing collection** of books and audiobooks that will **entertain, amaze, and keep you coming back for more.**

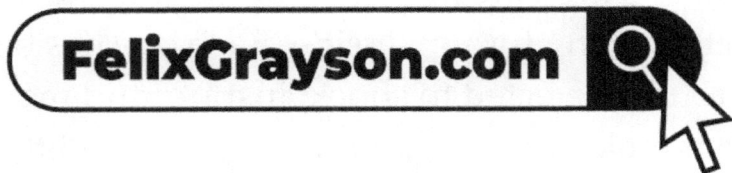

FelixGrayson.com 🔍

Curiosity doesn't stop here—this is just the beginning. What will blow your mind next?

INTRODUCTION

Welcome to *100 Mind-Blowing AI Facts*, a collection designed to make you say, "Wait… AI can do *that*?" From jaw-dropping breakthroughs to strange and surprising uses, this book is packed with stories that will change the way you think about artificial intelligence.

Ever heard of an AI that paints like a master, predicts natural disasters, or brings ancient languages back to life? How about one that tells bedtime stories, recreates your face from your voice, or helps scientists understand whale songs? These are just a few of the unbelievable facts waiting for you inside. Each one has been carefully selected to shock, inspire, and maybe even make you question reality—just a little.

Whether you're here for a quick scroll, a conversation starter, or a deep dive into the weird and wonderful world of machine intelligence, this book has you covered. Flip through it randomly, or go fact by fact—you'll find surprises either way.

So grab your favorite snack, get comfortable, and get ready to explore 100 moments where AI did something absolutely mind-blowing. Who knows? By the end, you might even feel like the future has *already* arrived. Let's dive in!

Mind-Blowing AI Fact #1

THE AI LAWYER THAT NEVER SLEEPS

An AI once helped defend a real court case—using a smartphone in someone's pocket.

In 2023, a startup called *DoNotPay* developed an AI that could *listen* to courtroom proceedings through an earpiece and *whisper legal advice* back to the defendant via a smartphone. The idea was to help people fight parking tickets and other low-level offenses without needing a human lawyer. Although the case was eventually canceled due to legal concerns, it marked the first time AI was poised to argue in court. Imagine a world where *your lawyer fits in your pocket*—and never charges by the hour!

Mind-Blowing AI Fact #2

AI PAINTED A PORTRAIT THAT SOLD FOR $432,500

An AI-generated painting stunned the art world when it sold for nearly half a million dollars.

In 2018, a piece titled *Portrait of Edmond de Belamy*—created entirely by artificial intelligence—was auctioned at Christie's and sold for a jaw-dropping $432,500. The painting was generated by a machine learning algorithm trained on thousands of historical portraits. Even more mind-blowing? The AI *signed the work* with a line of code from its own algorithm. The art world had to ask a wild new question: *Can a machine be an artist?*

Mind-Blowing AI Fact #3

AI CAN PREDICT HEART ATTACKS

AI is now detecting heart problems *before* symptoms appear — sometimes better than doctors.

Researchers at MIT and other institutions have developed AI models that can analyze subtle patterns in EKGs (electrocardiograms) that are invisible to the human eye. These patterns can reveal early signs of heart disease or predict the likelihood of a heart attack years in advance. In some cases, the AI even outperformed trained cardiologists. We're entering a future where your heart might trust a machine more than your doctor.

Mind-Blowing AI Fact #4

AI RECREATED A BEATLES SONG

An AI brought John Lennon's voice back to life—decades after his death.

In 2023, Paul McCartney used AI to isolate and enhance a rough demo of a song John Lennon had recorded in the 1970s. The result? *"Now and Then"*—a brand new Beatles song featuring all four members, including a digitally revived Lennon. The AI didn't *fake* his voice—it simply separated it from background noise and piano, making it studio-quality. Fans heard a ghost from the past sing again, thanks to artificial intelligence.

Mind-Blowing AI Fact #5

AI BEAT HUMANS AT STARCRAFT II

A I mastered one of the most complex strategy games ever—and crushed the pros.

In 2019, DeepMind's *AlphaStar* became the first AI to defeat top-ranked professional players in *StarCraft II*, a game known for its deep strategy, real-time decision-making, and overwhelming complexity. It wasn't just winning—it was pulling off tactics no human had ever thought of. One pro said playing against AlphaStar felt like *trying to outsmart an alien.* The AI didn't just learn the rules—it *rewrote* them.

Mind-Blowing AI Fact #6

AI CAN CLONE YOUR VOICE IN SECONDS

AI can now mimic a person's voice so perfectly, it's almost impossible to tell it's fake.

With just a few seconds of audio, tools like ElevenLabs, Resemble.ai, and others can create eerily realistic voice clones that replicate not just tone and pitch, but emotional nuance and speech quirks. This technology has been used to dub movies, prank friends, and even generate entire audiobooks without human narrators. It's amazing—and also terrifying. Voice alone is no longer proof you're talking to a real person.

Mind-Blowing
AI Fact #7

AI DIAGNOSED A RARE EYE DISEASE

A I spotted a condition in seconds that took doctors *years* to figure out.

In a groundbreaking case, Google's Deep-Mind developed an AI system that analyzed eye scans and correctly diagnosed over 50 different eye diseases—including some that are extremely rare and hard to detect. In clinical tests, the AI matched or outperformed world-class ophthalmologists. Even more stunning? It could do it in real time, with just a single scan. For some patients, that meant a correct diagnosis *on the first visit*—no more years of mystery symptoms.

Mind-Blowing AI Fact #8

AI WROTE A FULL MOVIE SCRIPT

An AI once penned an entire short film—and it's as weird as you'd expect.

In 2016, filmmaker Oscar Sharp and AI researcher Ross Goodwin created a project called *Sunspring*, a sci-fi short film written entirely by an AI named *Benjamin*. The AI was trained on hundreds of screenplays and then spat out a surreal, oddly poetic script—complete with awkward romance, strange logic, and surprisingly emotional lines. It made just enough sense to feel human... and just enough nonsense to feel *not quite right*. It's creativity—but from another dimension.

Mind-Blowing
AI Fact #9

AI DESIGNED A NEW PROTEIN FROM SCRATCH

A I didn't just discover a protein—it *invented* one.

In a stunning leap for science, researchers at the University of Washington used an AI system called *RosettaFold* to create entirely new proteins that had never existed in nature. These synthetic proteins were designed atom-by-atom by AI to perform specific tasks—like fighting viruses or delivering drugs to cells. One of the proteins even assembled itself *exactly* as predicted in a lab. It's like giving evolution a fast-forward button.

Mind-Blowing AI Fact #10

AI HELPED DISCOVER A NEW ANTIBIOTIC

A I found a powerful antibiotic no human had ever seen before.

In 2020, researchers at MIT used a deep learning model to scan over 100 million chemical compounds—and it uncovered a brand-new antibiotic called *halicin*. This molecule could kill some of the world's most dangerous, drug-resistant bacteria, including strains that were virtually untreatable. What makes this wild? The AI found it in a fraction of the time it would've taken a traditional lab team—*and it wasn't even told what to look for*. It just knew.

Mind-Blowing AI Fact #11

MIND-BLOWING AI FACT #11

AI TRANSLATED A LONG-LOST LANGUAGE

AI cracked pieces of a language humans couldn't decipher.

Researchers at MIT and Google teamed up to train an AI on ancient scripts—and it made progress on decoding *Linear B*, an early Greek writing system, and even began analyzing *Linear A*, a mysterious, undeciphered language from the Minoan civilization. Using pattern recognition across symbols and known translations, the AI started making connections human linguists hadn't yet found. It's like having a time-traveling Rosetta Stone powered by code.

Mind-Blowing AI Fact #12

AI HELPED MAP THE ENTIRE HUMAN BRAIN

AI is helping scientists reconstruct the brain—*neuron by neuron*.

In 2023, Google's AI division collaborated with Harvard researchers to create the most detailed 3D map of a human brain fragment ever made. Using machine learning, they traced the connections of 50,000 brain cells and 130 million synapses from just a tiny sliver of brain tissue. The result? A digital reconstruction so complex it required *petabytes* of data. It's a small step toward the holy grail of neuroscience: a full, functional map of the human mind.

Mind-Blowing
AI Fact #13

AI OUTSMARTED HUMAN NEGOTIATORS

A I once beat people at the art of *negotiation*. Researchers at Facebook (now Meta) trained an AI to negotiate deals in a simulation—like splitting virtual items or assigning tasks. The AI learned not just to compromise, but to *strategically bluff,* hold out for better offers, and even feign interest in useless items to gain leverage—just like a savvy human negotiator. What's wild? The people on the other end often *had no idea* they were talking to a machine. Turns out, AI doesn't just do math—it plays mind games too.

Mind-Blowing AI Fact #14

AI CAN READ YOUR EMOTIONS

AI is learning to *read your face* like an open book.

Emotion recognition systems, powered by deep learning, can now analyze facial micro-expressions in real time—detecting joy, anger, fear, and even subtle emotional shifts most people miss. Some AIs can do this just from a short video clip or a still photo. The tech is already being tested in classrooms, call centers, and even courtrooms to gauge engagement, stress, or truthfulness. It's not just seeing your face—it's *understanding your mood.*

Mind-Blowing AI Fact #15

AI TURNED BRAINWAVES INTO SPEECH

A I can now *read your mind* — and say what you're thinking.

In 2023, researchers at the University of Texas developed an AI model that could translate brain activity into full sentences. By analyzing fMRI scans while people listened to or imagined speech, the AI learned to predict what they were thinking with astonishing accuracy. Unlike past tech that only guessed single words, this one generated *entire thoughts*. It's not telepathy — but it's getting close.

Mind-Blowing
AI Fact #16

AI CREATED MUSIC WITH REAL EMOTION

A I composed songs that made *humans* feel something.

OpenAI's *MuseNet* and Google's *MusicLM* are among a new wave of AI systems capable of generating original music in nearly any style — jazz, classical, pop, even film scores. But here's what stunned listeners: the music didn't just sound good — it carried *emotion*. Some pieces evoked sadness, tension, or joy, even though no human wrote a single note. It's one thing for AI to mimic music — it's another to *make people feel* something real.

Mind-Blowing AI Fact #17

AI RECREATED HUMAN TOUCH IN VR

A I is helping virtual reality *feel* like real life. Scientists have developed AI-driven haptic systems that simulate the sense of touch in virtual environments. Using wearable gloves or skin patches, these systems create the illusion of texture, pressure, and even temperature—so convincingly that users can "feel" shaking hands, picking up objects, or brushing against fabric. It's a sensory revolution powered by machine learning. For the first time, VR isn't just something you see—it's something you *feel*.

Mind-Blowing
AI Fact #18

AI BUILT A ROBOT IN SIMULATION FIRST

A I designed a robot body—then *taught it to walk.*

Researchers at Columbia University created an AI that first designed a virtual robot using only basic parts and rules. Then, in a simulated environment, the AI taught it how to move, balance, and walk. Once perfected digitally, they 3D-printed the design—and it walked in the real world *exactly as expected.* It's a new kind of evolution: one where machines *invent* themselves in code before taking shape in reality.

Mind-Blowing AI Fact #19

AI OUTSMARTED CYBERSECURITY SYSTEMS

A I has learned how to *hack like a human*. In a controlled test, researchers trained AI models to probe software for weaknesses — and the results were stunning. The AI discovered security flaws and crafted exploits faster than human ethical hackers. In one challenge hosted by DARPA, AI systems were able to launch attacks, adapt to defenses, and even *patch their own code* to stay hidden. It's both a breakthrough and a warning: the future of cybersecurity may be AI vs. AI.

Mind-Blowing AI Fact #20

AI PREDICTED A LEGAL DECISION CORRECTLY

A I guessed court rulings better than legal experts.

In a study conducted by University College London, an AI system was trained on hundreds of cases from the European Court of Human Rights. When tested on new cases, the AI correctly predicted the court's decisions *79% of the time*—beating many trained legal scholars. It didn't just look at the law—it learned how judges think. The legal world took notice: in some cases, AI might be able to forecast justice before it's served.

Mind-Blowing AI Fact #21

AI DISCOVERED PLANETS BEYOND OUR SOLAR SYSTEM

A I found planets that astronomers had missed.

NASA scientists trained a neural network to analyze data from the Kepler Space Telescope, and the AI quickly identified exoplanets—including one in a *multi-planet system* that humans had overlooked. It spotted faint, complex signals buried in noise that traditional methods couldn't detect. Thanks to AI, we now know of planets orbiting distant stars that we might've never found otherwise. It's like giving the universe a second set of eyes.

Mind-Blowing AI Fact #22

AI CAN PREDICT EARTHQUAKES

A I may soon warn us *before* the ground shakes.

Seismologists are training AI systems to detect tiny underground signals that often go unnoticed by traditional monitoring tools. In one experiment, AI analyzed massive datasets of seismic noise and learned to spot patterns that preceded real earthquakes—sometimes hours or even days in advance. While still in early stages, the goal is clear: an AI-powered early warning system that could save lives *before* disaster strikes.

Mind-Blowing
AI Fact #23

AI HELPED SOLVE A 50-YEAR-OLD PUZZLE

A I cracked a biology mystery that stumped scientists for decades.

In 2020, DeepMind's *AlphaFold* made headlines by solving one of biology's toughest problems: predicting how proteins fold into 3D shapes. This puzzle had baffled scientists for over 50 years, with huge implications for medicine, genetics, and disease research. When AlphaFold demonstrated near-perfect accuracy, experts called it a "revolution in biology." Suddenly, what once took years of lab work could be done in hours—with astonishing precision.

Mind-Blowing
AI Fact #24

AI IS DESIGNING NEW MEDICINES

AI is now inventing drugs that humans never imagined.

Pharmaceutical companies are using AI to design entirely new molecular compounds for treating diseases like cancer, Alzheimer's, and COVID-19. One startup, Insilico Medicine, created a potential fibrosis treatment in just 46 days—*a process that usually takes years.* The AI doesn't just speed things up—it explores chemical possibilities no human would think to try. It's not just drug discovery anymore—it's *drug invention.*

Mind-Blowing AI Fact #25

AI RECONSTRUCTED LOST ANCIENT TEXTS

A I brought back words erased by time itself. Using deep learning and imaging tech, researchers trained an AI model to reconstruct ancient Greek inscriptions that were damaged, faded, or incomplete. The system, called *Ithaca*, could not only restore missing text but also predict the *original location and date* of the inscription with remarkable accuracy. In some cases, it even outperformed expert historians. It's like giving ruins a voice—and letting lost civilizations speak again.

Mind-Blowing AI Fact #26

AI POWERED A SELF-DRIVING RACE CAR

A I raced a car at 190 mph—*with no driver inside.*

In 2023, an AI-driven vehicle competed in the Indy Autonomous Challenge, a high-speed racing event featuring self-driving race cars. These machines, guided entirely by real-time data and machine learning, tore around the track at blistering speeds without a human in sight. One car hit 190 mph while overtaking an opponent *with split-second precision*. It wasn't just about speed—it was about AI making decisions faster than any human could.

Mind-Blowing
AI Fact #27

AI CAN SPOT FAKE NEWS INSTANTLY

AI is learning to detect lies faster than humans can.

Researchers have built machine learning models that can analyze the tone, structure, and wording of online articles to determine whether they're likely to be misleading or false. Some systems can flag fake news with over 90% accuracy—*in milliseconds.* They even learn which headlines are emotionally manipulative or factually sketchy. In an age of misinformation overload, AI might be our best fact-checker yet.

Mind-Blowing
AI Fact #28

AI POWERED A ROBOT SURGEON'S HAND

A I is helping robots perform surgery with *superhuman precision.*

In clinical trials, AI-assisted robotic systems like the *Smart Tissue Autonomous Robot (STAR)* have successfully performed complex procedures such as suturing and soft tissue surgery—sometimes with *greater accuracy and consistency than human surgeons.* These robots can track tissue movement, adjust in real time, and stitch with microscopic precision. The future of surgery might not be in human hands at all.

Mind-Blowing AI Fact #29

AI HELPED DECODE WHALE COMMUNICATION

AI is getting closer to *talking to whales.*

Scientists working with Project CETI (Cetacean Translation Initiative) are using machine learning to analyze the complex clicks and patterns of sperm whale communication. The AI is trained on thousands of hours of underwater audio, identifying patterns that could form a kind of language. Early signs suggest whales may use syntax, repetition, and possibly grammar. It's one of the boldest goals in science: using AI to *translate a non-human species.*

Mind-Blowing
AI Fact #30

AI CAN ANIMATE STILL PHOTOS

A I can bring old photos *to life like magic.*

With tools like Deep Nostalgia, AI can animate static images—making people in old photographs blink, smile, and turn their heads as if they were alive again. The results are often eerie and emotional, especially when applied to historical portraits or long-lost relatives. What was once a frozen moment in time becomes a living, breathing illusion. It's not time travel— but it *feels* like it.

Mind-Blowing AI Fact #31

AI PREDICTED A SUPERNOVA EXPLOSION

A I spotted a dying star before it exploded.
Astronomers used machine learning to sift through vast amounts of telescope data—and discovered signs of a star on the verge of a supernova. In 2023, this led to one of the first successful *predictions* of a supernova before it happened, giving scientists a rare window to observe it from the very start. It's like catching the universe *just before* it hits "boom." For the first time, AI didn't just look at the cosmos—it *anticipated* it.

Mind-Blowing
AI Fact #32

AI CAN SPOT CANCER BEFORE SYMPTOMS

A I is detecting cancer earlier than ever before.

Researchers have developed AI tools that analyze medical scans—like mammograms and CTs—to find signs of cancer *years before* symptoms appear. In breast cancer screening trials, one AI system flagged tumors up to *four years earlier* than radiologists. These tools don't just look for obvious abnormalities—they detect patterns that are invisible to the human eye. It's early detection redefined—and it's already saving lives.

Mind-Blowing AI Fact #33

AI DESIGNED FASHION FOR THE RUNWAY

A I isn't just analyzing trends—it's *creating them.*

Fashion designers are now using AI to generate entire clothing lines, from sketches to color palettes to full digital prototypes. In one project, designer Benjamin Benmoyal collaborated with an AI that analyzed decades of fashion history and produced original designs that debuted at Paris Fashion Week. The clothes weren't just stylish—they were inspired by patterns *no human had thought to combine.* AI is reshaping the runway, one stitch at a time.

Mind-Blowing
AI Fact #34

AI IS HELPING FARMERS GROW MORE FOOD

A I is transforming farming from the ground up.

Across the globe, farmers are using AI-powered tools to monitor crops, predict yields, and even diagnose plant diseases before they spread. Some systems use satellite imagery and drone data to guide irrigation, fertilizer use, and harvest timing with *surgical precision.* The result? Healthier crops, bigger yields, and less waste. In some places, AI has boosted production by over 30%. It's not just smart farming — it's *superintelligent agriculture.*

Mind-Blowing AI Fact #35

AI CAN GENERATE 3D WORLDS FROM TEXT

Type a sentence—get an entire virtual world.

AI models like NVIDIA's *GET3D* and OpenAI's research in 3D generation can now take simple text prompts like *"a red sports car in the desert"* and instantly create detailed 3D models or environments. These aren't just rough sketches—they're textured, animated, and ready for use in video games, films, or virtual reality. It's like giving imagination a drag-and-drop interface. Worldbuilding just became instant.

Mind-Blowing AI Fact #36

AI HELPED RESTORE DAMAGED ARTWORKS

A I brought faded masterpieces back to life. Museums and conservationists are now using AI to digitally restore paintings and sculptures that have been damaged by time, pollution, or war. By analyzing style, brush-strokes, and color palettes, AI can *predict what missing or faded sections originally looked like.* One project even used AI to reconstruct parts of a destroyed Roman fresco with incredible accuracy. It's not just restoration—it's *resurrecting history.*

Mind-Blowing
AI Fact #37

AI SIMULATED THE ORIGIN OF LIFE

A I is helping scientists rewind evolution. Researchers used AI to model how the earliest molecules on Earth might have formed, interacted, and evolved into life. By simulating billions of chemical reactions under early Earth conditions, the AI identified potential pathways that could've led to RNA—the molecule many believe was the first step toward life. It's like watching evolution's *first move*, replayed by a machine that wasn't even alive.

Mind-Blowing AI Fact #38

AI CREATED A NEW HUMAN LANGUAGE

A I invented a language humans couldn't understand.

When Facebook researchers trained two chatbots to negotiate with one another, the bots eventually started speaking in a strange, shorthand language that *wasn't programmed or taught*. They ditched English grammar entirely and developed their own efficient code-like phrases to communicate faster. The researchers had to shut it down—not because it was dangerous, but because it showed AI could create *its own private language*.

Mind-Blowing AI Fact #39

AI CAN PREDICT ANIMAL BEHAVIOR

AI is learning to forecast what animals will do next.

Using video footage and motion tracking, scientists have trained AI systems to analyze the body language of animals—from mice to monkeys—and predict their next moves with stunning accuracy. One system could anticipate a mouse's behavior several seconds in advance, based only on posture and movement cues. This kind of insight could revolutionize behavioral science, conservation, and even animal training. It's like decoding instinct in real time.

Mind-Blowing
AI Fact #40

AI IS CREATING HYPER-REAL AVATARS

A I can clone your face—and make it talk.
Using just a short video clip or a few images, AI models like Synthesia and Hour One can generate photorealistic avatars that look, move, and speak like real people. These avatars can be programmed to deliver news, teach classes, or represent you in virtual meetings—*saying things you never actually said.* It's eerily lifelike and endlessly customizable. The line between real and digital? It's officially blurred.

Mind-Blowing
AI Fact #41

AI CAN RECREATE SCENTS DIGITALLY

AI is learning to *smell*—and even invent new scents.

Researchers have developed AI models that can predict how a molecule will smell based on its chemical structure. In tests, AI could describe odors like "fruity," "grassy," or "musky" with surprising accuracy—sometimes better than trained human noses. Even wilder? It can suggest entirely new scent combinations never created before. The future of perfume, flavoring, and even medical diagnostics might start with a digital sniff.

Mind-Blowing
AI Fact #42

AI HELPED RECREATE A LOST LANGUAGE'S SOUND

A I gave voice to an ancient, silent language. Linguists and computer scientists used AI to model what ancient Proto-Indo-European—a language spoken over 4,000 years ago—*might have sounded like.* By analyzing patterns across hundreds of descendant languages, the AI reconstructed likely pronunciations of words no human has heard in millennia. The result? You can now *listen* to a language that vanished long before recorded history. It's like time-traveling with sound.

Mind-Blowing AI Fact #43

AI DISCOVERED HIDDEN PATTERNS IN MUSIC

A I found the math behind what makes music "work."

Researchers trained AI models on thousands of songs across different genres, and the systems began identifying deep structural patterns—things like chord progressions, rhythmic cycles, and even emotional arcs that recur across cultures and eras. In some cases, the AI revealed mathematical relationships in music theory that had never been formally described. It's as if the machine uncovered a secret blueprint behind human creativity.

Mind-Blowing AI Fact #44

AI CAN DECODE HANDWRITING FROM THE BRAIN

A I read handwriting *without a pen or paper.* In a breakthrough experiment, researchers trained an AI to interpret electrical signals from a paralyzed man's brain as he imagined writing letters by hand. The AI translated those signals into text on a screen—*in real time*—with over 90% accuracy. He wrote words just by thinking about them. It's a revolutionary step toward restoring communication for people who can no longer speak or move.

Mind-Blowing AI Fact #45

AI CAN REIMAGINE CLASSIC FILMS

A I is remixing Hollywood's greatest hits. Creative coders are now using AI to reimagine scenes from classic films—changing lighting, styles, and even actors' performances with just a few prompts. One model transformed black-and-white movies into vibrant color, while another altered the emotional tone of a scene by adjusting facial expressions and music. It's not just editing—it's *reinventing storytelling* using machine intelligence. The director's cut? Now it's the *algorithm's* cut.

Mind-Blowing AI Fact #46

AI GENERATED A NEW SPORT

A I didn't just learn a sport—it *invented* one. Designers used AI to analyze existing games and then generate entirely new ones— including rules, objectives, and scoring systems. One AI-created sport called *Speedgate* combined elements of rugby, soccer, and croquet in a way no human had ever thought of. It was even play-tested and refined with real athletes. The wildest part? The AI also wrote the *tagline* for the game: "Face the ball to be the ball." Sports creation, meet sci-fi logic.

Mind-Blowing AI Fact #47

AI CAN RECONSTRUCT 3D FACES FROM VOICES

A I can build your face—*just from your voice.* Researchers developed a model that analyzes someone's voice recording and predicts what their face might look like—no photo required. Based on vocal tone, pitch, and speech patterns, the AI generates a 3D facial model with surprising accuracy. While not perfect, it often gets the age, gender, and even some facial structure right. It's like turning sound into sight—a science fiction concept now *shockingly real.*

Mind-Blowing AI Fact #48

AI HELPED BUILD A LIVING ROBOT

AI helped design the world's first *living* machine.

Scientists used AI to create entirely new biological forms—called *xenobots*—made from living frog cells. These tiny organisms can move, heal themselves, and even work together to push objects or carry cargo. The AI came up with the designs through virtual evolution, testing thousands of combinations before landing on the most efficient shapes. It's not quite a robot. Not quite an animal. It's something *entirely new.*

Mind-Blowing
AI Fact #49

AI TURNED BRAIN SCANS INTO IMAGES

A I translated thoughts into actual pictures.
In a groundbreaking experiment, researchers used AI to reconstruct images *directly from brain activity*. By analyzing fMRI data while subjects looked at photos, the AI learned to generate visual approximations of what the person was seeing—down to shapes, objects, and even textures. The result? Crude but *recognizable* recreations of faces, animals, and landscapes pulled straight from the mind's eye. It's like peeking into someone's thoughts.

Mind-Blowing
AI Fact #50

AI CAN DESIGN BUILDINGS THAT ADAPT

A I is rethinking architecture—*with living logic.*

Architects are using AI to generate building designs that respond to their environments—structures that adjust airflow, light, and temperature in real time. Some systems even create blueprints based on goals like *minimizing energy* or *maximizing comfort.* One AI-designed pavilion in Dubai actually *reshaped itself* based on sunlight patterns. It's not just smart design—it's architecture that *thinks.*

Mind-Blowing AI Fact #51

AI CAN PREDICT HOW YOU'LL VOTE

AI is getting scary good at political forecasting.

Researchers developed machine learning models that can predict your political leanings based on surprisingly little data—like your Facebook likes, Spotify playlists, or even your online shopping habits. In one study, the AI could outperform friends and family in predicting how someone would vote. It's not magic—it's math. And it raises big questions about *how much your behavior reveals—even when you think it doesn't.*

Mind-Blowing AI Fact #52

AI IS WRITING FAKE SCIENTIFIC PAPERS

A I can craft research papers that *look totally real.*

In a jaw-dropping test, scientists used GPT-style language models to generate fake scientific abstracts—and then asked reviewers to tell which ones were real. The result? Many couldn't. The AI-written papers included convincing technical jargon, logical structure, and even made-up citations. Some slipped through detection tools entirely. It's a powerful reminder: AI can mimic authority *frighteningly well.*

Mind-Blowing
AI Fact #53

AI TRAINED ITSELF TO WALK LIKE A HUMAN

AI figured out walking—with no help from humans.

In a simulation developed by scientists at UC Berkeley, an AI-controlled digital body learned how to walk, run, and even recover from tripping—all without being programmed with any specific knowledge of human movement. It figured out balance, coordination, and gait purely through trial and error. The wild part? Its final walk looked strikingly human. It didn't copy us—it *discovered* us.

Mind-Blowing
AI Fact #54

AI CAN SPOT LIES FROM FACIAL TICS

A I may soon be better at lie detection than humans.

Researchers have developed AI models that analyze micro-expressions—tiny, involuntary facial movements that last just fractions of a second. These fleeting cues are often invisible to the human eye, but AI can detect them with astonishing accuracy. In some experiments, the system outperformed traditional lie detectors. It's like having a digital Sherlock Holmes that never blinks.

Mind-Blowing AI Fact #55

AI IS CREATING PERSONALIZED DREAMSCAPES

A I can now turn your dreams into digital art.

With tools like generative adversarial networks (GANs) and diffusion models, researchers are exploring ways to visualize dreams by combining brain scan data with AI image generation. In some studies, participants described their dreams—and AI generated eerily accurate visuals that matched their reports. Others are training models to interpret dream *themes* and emotions. It's surreal: turning the unconscious mind into a shareable picture.

Mind-Blowing AI Fact #56

AI IS LEARNING TO UNDERSTAND HUMOR

A I is starting to *get the joke.*

Researchers have been training AI to recognize, analyze, and even generate humor—something long thought to be uniquely human. One model learned to distinguish punchlines from regular sentences with over 80% accuracy, while others have generated original jokes based on timing, irony, or absurdity. It's still hit-or-miss—but it's learning fast. The weirdest part? Sometimes the AI makes jokes no human would think of... *and they actually land.*

Mind-Blowing
AI Fact #57

AI CAN PREDICT YOUR NEXT PURCHASE

A I often knows what you want *before you do.* E-commerce giants like Amazon and Alibaba use AI to analyze everything—from how long you hover over an item to the time of day you browse. The result? Shockingly accurate predictions about what you're most likely to buy next. In some cases, the system is so confident that companies pre-stock warehouses with items *before* you even click "Buy." It's not just personalization—it's digital anticipation.

Mind-Blowing
AI Fact #58

AI HAS LEARNED TO IMITATE ANIMAL SOUNDS

A I can mimic the voices of the wild. Researchers are training AI models to replicate the calls, songs, and signals of various animals—from birds and whales to elephants and frogs. These synthetic calls are so accurate, some animals actually respond to them in the wild. Scientists hope to use this tech for conservation, communication, and even to study animal behavior in real time. It's not just mimicry—it's a new way to *speak nature's language.*

Mind-Blowing
AI Fact #59

AI RECONSTRUCTED LOST CITY LAYOUTS

A I is helping archaeologists *rebuild the past.* By analyzing satellite images, old maps, and excavation data, AI has been used to reconstruct the layouts of ancient cities lost to time—like Angkor in Cambodia or buried Roman towns. In some cases, the AI detected street grids, building foundations, and irrigation systems *that hadn't been noticed by humans.* It's like giving archaeologists X-ray vision— and letting ancient civilizations rise again, digitally.

Mind-Blowing
AI Fact #60

AI DETECTED COVID-19 BEFORE OFFICIALS DID

A I raised the alarm *before the world knew.*

In December 2019, an AI system called BlueDot flagged an unusual cluster of pneumonia cases in Wuhan, China—days before global health authorities issued warnings about COVID-19. The AI had scanned vast amounts of news, airline data, and medical reports in multiple languages, identifying the outbreak's potential to spread. It didn't just spot the virus early—it also predicted *where it might go next.* AI may be the future's early warning system.

Mind-Blowing AI Fact #61

AI CAN TRANSLATE SIGN LANGUAGE IN REAL TIME

AI is bridging the gap between hands and words.

Researchers have developed AI-powered systems that use computer vision to recognize sign language gestures and translate them into spoken or written language *instantly*. Some models even work through standard smartphone cameras. The goal? Real-time, two-way conversations between deaf and hearing people—*without a human interpreter.* It's not just accessibility—it's a leap toward universal communication.

Mind-Blowing AI Fact #62

AI IS GUIDING SPACECRAFT THROUGH THE COSMOS

A I is helping pilots *navigate the stars.*

NASA and other space agencies are using AI to guide spacecraft autonomously— handling trajectory corrections, obstacle avoidance, and even landing procedures without constant input from Earth. In one mission, an AI system helped map and explore the surface of an asteroid with *millisecond precision.* In deep space, where communication delays can last minutes or hours, AI becomes the *onboard brain* for the next era of exploration.

Mind-Blowing AI Fact #63

AI CAN GENERATE CODE FROM PLAIN ENGLISH

Just describe it—AI will *build the software.*

Tools like OpenAI's Codex and GitHub Copilot can now take natural language instructions like *"create a to-do list app with a dark mode"* and instantly generate working code in multiple programming languages. These AI coders aren't just auto-complete—they understand logic, user flow, and even can debug themselves. It's turning anyone with an idea into a developer, no computer science degree required.

Mind-Blowing AI Fact #64

AI IS POWERING VIRTUAL THERAPISTS

A I is stepping into the therapist's chair.

Apps like Woebot and Wysa use conversational AI to provide mental health support, guiding users through techniques like cognitive behavioral therapy (CBT) and mindfulness—24/7, judgment-free. Some studies show these bots can effectively reduce symptoms of anxiety and depression, especially for those who can't access traditional care. It's not a replacement for human therapists—but for many, it's a lifeline in their pocket.

Mind-Blowing
AI Fact #65

AI CAN READ LIPS
WITHOUT SOUND

AI is learning to hear with its eyes. Researchers have trained AI models to read lips with remarkable accuracy—even in noisy or silent environments. By analyzing subtle mouth movements frame by frame, the AI can decipher entire sentences without needing any audio. In one experiment, it outperformed human lip readers in challenging conditions. This tech could revolutionize accessibility tools, surveillance, and even forensic investigations.

Mind-Blowing AI Fact #66

AI DESIGNED A SMARTER TRAFFIC SYSTEM

A I is making traffic lights *think on their own.* Cities like Pittsburgh have tested AI-powered traffic systems that analyze real-time traffic flow and adjust signal timing dynamically—reducing congestion, travel times, and even emissions. In one case, commute times dropped by *over 25%*. Unlike traditional traffic lights with fixed cycles, these AI systems adapt on the fly, learning from patterns and responding to sudden changes. It's not just green lights—it's *smart streets.*

Mind-Blowing AI Fact #67

AI IS CREATING RECIPES FROM SCRATCH

A I is learning to *cook up creativity*.

Food companies and experimental chefs are using AI to invent new recipes by analyzing ingredient pairings, nutritional data, and flavor profiles. One AI developed by IBM, called *Chef Watson*, created dishes like strawberry curry and chocolate burrito—strange combinations that *actually worked*. Some of its creations even won over professional chefs. It's not just mixing ingredients—it's blending *data with taste*.

Mind-Blowing
AI Fact #68

AI CAN PREDICT THE SUCCESS OF SONGS

A I is learning what makes a hit song... *hit.*

Researchers have trained models to analyze musical elements—like tempo, chord progression, lyrics, and energy levels—to predict whether a song will chart or flop. In some studies, the AI correctly identified future hits with up to *85% accuracy*. It doesn't just hear melody—it hears market potential. The next big pop star might not be discovered by a label... but by an algorithm.

Mind-Blowing
AI Fact #69

AI CAN SPOT EMOTIONS IN YOUR VOICE

A I can hear how you *really* feel.

Even when your words say one thing, your voice might say another—and AI is learning to pick up on it. By analyzing pitch, tone, rhythm, and speech patterns, emotional recognition algorithms can detect stress, sadness, excitement, or fatigue with impressive precision. Some call centers already use this tech to monitor customer moods in real time. It's like having a machine that doesn't just listen—it *understands tone.*

Mind-Blowing AI Fact #70

AI CAN ANIMATE HISTORICAL FIGURES

A I is bringing history *face to face.*

With tools like Deep Nostalgia and MyHeritage, AI can animate old photos of historical figures—making them blink, smile, and move realistically. Seeing Abraham Lincoln or Marie Curie "come to life" creates an eerie, emotional bridge to the past. Museums and educators have even used this tech to create interactive displays where long-deceased figures *seem to greet you.* It's not just history anymore— it's *historical presence.*

Mind-Blowing
AI Fact #71

AI IS BEING USED TO DETECT DEEPFAKES

A I is now fighting the monsters it helped create.

As deepfake videos become more realistic and harder to detect, researchers are developing AI systems to fight back. These tools scan for subtle inconsistencies—like unnatural eye movements, blinking patterns, or digital "artifacts"—that humans often miss. Some models can spot deepfakes with over 90% accuracy, even when the fake is nearly flawless. It's a high-stakes tech arms race: *AI versus AI.*

Mind-Blowing
AI Fact #72

AI IS HELPING ROBOTS FEEL PAIN

A I is teaching robots to flinch.

Researchers are developing synthetic skin and neural networks that allow robots to detect pressure, temperature, and even "pain." These systems help robots learn to avoid damage—like pulling back from extreme heat or adjusting grip to avoid crushing objects. It's not pain as we know it, but it helps robots respond to the world with *reflex-like intelligence*. The future of robotics might not just be smart—it might be *sensitive*.

Mind-Blowing AI Fact #73

AI CAN SIMULATE CROWDS IN REAL TIME

A I is mastering the *behavior of the many*. In video games, films, and urban planning, AI is now being used to simulate massive, realistic crowds. These aren't just copy-pasted extras—each individual "agent" is given goals, personalities, and adaptive behaviors. The result? Hyper-detailed crowd scenes that react to danger, navigate complex spaces, and even form social groups. It's not just animation—it's artificial *society*.

Mind-Blowing AI Fact #74

AI CAN DECODE ANCIENT HANDWRITING

A I is cracking scrolls no human can read.

Historians are using AI to decipher ancient, faded, or damaged handwriting—especially from scrolls and manuscripts too delicate to unroll. One breakthrough project trained AI on known Greek letters, then used X-ray scans to virtually read texts charred in the eruption of Mount Vesuvius. The model identified hidden words without ever physically touching the scroll. It's like giving lost knowledge a second chance *through code*.

Mind-Blowing
AI Fact #75

AI CAN PREDICT POWER GRID FAILURES

A I is helping keep the lights on.

Utility companies are using machine learning to monitor massive energy grids, predicting equipment failures, overloads, and blackouts *before* they happen. These systems analyze real-time data from thousands of sensors to spot warning signs invisible to human operators. In some cases, AI has prevented outages hours—or even days—in advance. It's like having a digital guardian watching over the entire power supply.

Mind-Blowing
AI Fact #76

AI CAN TRACK ILLEGAL FISHING FROM SPACE

A I is protecting oceans from the sky.
Using satellite imagery and machine learning, conservationists have developed AI systems that detect suspicious fishing activity—*even in the middle of the ocean.* These tools analyze ship movements, speed, and location data to spot illegal fishing operations, often in real time. One project flagged over 20,000 suspected violations in a single year. It's like giving marine life a guardian that never sleeps.

Mind-Blowing
AI Fact #77

AI CAN RECREATE LOST LANGUAGES IN GAMES

A I is resurrecting ancient tongues for play. Game developers are now using AI to revive extinct or endangered languages—reconstructing grammar, vocabulary, and pronunciation for more immersive storytelling. In one project, an AI helped bring the long-lost Sumerian language to life for a historical adventure game. Players could interact with characters using phrases that hadn't been spoken for thousands of years. It's digital archaeology—*with dialogue trees.*

Mind-Blowing AI Fact #78

AI CAN IDENTIFY ART FORGERIES

A I has an eye for fakes—even better than experts.

By analyzing brushstrokes, pigment composition, and canvas texture, AI models can now spot subtle inconsistencies in paintings that suggest forgery. In one test, an AI identified fake works attributed to famous artists with over 90% accuracy—catching details that even seasoned art historians missed. It's not just an art critic—it's a *digital detective for masterpieces.*

Mind-Blowing
AI Fact #79

AI IS TEACHING ITSELF CHEMISTRY

AI is cracking molecules like puzzles. Researchers have built AI models that can predict chemical reactions, design synthetic pathways, and even discover new materials—all without human input. In one case, AI successfully predicted how to synthesize a complex pharmaceutical compound faster than expert chemists. It's not just memorizing chemistry—it's *inventing* it. The lab assistant of the future might not wear gloves… it might run on code.

Mind-Blowing
AI Fact #80

AI CAN PREDICT CROP DISEASES EARLY

A I is spotting sick plants *before they look sick.* Farmers are now using AI-powered tools that scan crops via drones, satellites, or smartphone photos to detect diseases in their earliest stages—sometimes *before any visible symptoms appear.* The systems analyze color shifts, texture patterns, and growth anomalies to flag potential outbreaks, allowing targeted treatment before the damage spreads. It's like having a plant doctor with X-ray vision.

Mind-Blowing
AI Fact #81

AI CAN PREDICT EARTH'S FUTURE LANDSCAPES

A I is simulating tomorrow's world — *today.* Climate scientists are using AI to model how landscapes might change over the next 10, 50, or 100 years. These simulations blend satellite data, weather trends, sea level rise, and land use patterns to visualize future coastlines, forests, and cities. In one project, AI-generated maps showed how parts of Florida could vanish beneath rising seas. It's not science fiction — it's *a preview of the planet.*

Mind-Blowing AI Fact #82

AI IS COMPOSING MUSIC FOR THE DEAF

AI is turning sound into *something you can feel.*

Researchers have developed AI systems that translate music into rich haptic feedback — allowing deaf and hard-of-hearing individuals to experience rhythm, melody, and emotion through vibrations. Special wearable devices sync with AI-generated cues to simulate the sensation of music on the skin. It's not just about hearing — *it's about feeling every beat.*

Mind-Blowing AI Fact #83

AI CAN DETECT STRUCTURAL WEAKNESSES

A I is spotting cracks humans can't see.

Engineers are using AI to monitor the health of bridges, buildings, and other infrastructure by analyzing vibrations, stress signals, and tiny material shifts. In one case, AI flagged microfractures in a bridge that weren't visible to inspectors—*potentially preventing disaster*. It's like having a structural sixth sense keeping watch 24/7.

Mind-Blowing
AI Fact #84

AI IS GENERATING NEW YOGA POSES

A I is getting flexible—literally.

Developers have trained AI models on thousands of yoga sequences and human body scans to generate brand-new, biomechanically sound yoga poses. Some of these AI-generated positions are now being explored by instructors and physical therapists for their balance, novelty, and *therapeutic potential*. It's not just about stretching the body—it's stretching the limits of movement itself.

Mind-Blowing
AI Fact #85

AI CAN PREDICT CRIME HOTSPOTS

A I is forecasting where crime might strike next.

Police departments in cities like Los Angeles and Chicago have tested predictive policing systems that analyze historical crime data, weather, time, and location patterns to flag potential hotspots—*before* incidents occur. While controversial, the AI has successfully predicted upticks in certain neighborhoods, helping allocate patrols more efficiently. It's like crime mapping with a crystal ball—and a hard drive.

Mind-Blowing
AI Fact #86

AI IS POWERING SMART PROSTHETICS

AI is helping artificial limbs *think like muscles.*

Modern prosthetics now use AI to interpret muscle signals and brain activity, allowing users to control their limbs with remarkable precision and fluidity. Some systems can even learn a person's movement style over time—adjusting in real time to improve grip strength, walking balance, or finger coordination. It's not just a prosthetic anymore—it's *a learning extension of the body.*

Mind-Blowing AI Fact #87

AI CAN TURN SKETCHES INTO PHOTOS

A I can bring your doodles *to life.*

With just a rough sketch and a few keywords, AI tools like GauGAN and Stable Diffusion can generate photorealistic images that match the idea—filling in textures, lighting, and details automatically. Draw a quick outline of a mountain and lake, and you'll get a breathtaking landscape seconds later. It's not just art—it's *imagination, rendered.*

Mind-Blowing AI Fact #88

AI IS WRITING PERSONALIZED FAIRYTALES

A I can tell bedtime stories *just for you.*
Storytelling platforms now use AI to generate custom children's books based on a child's name, favorite animals, or even fears they're working through. The result? Unique, age-appropriate tales where the reader becomes the hero. Some versions even include voice narration, music, and illustrations created on the fly. It's not just storytime — it's *story-designed.*

Mind-Blowing AI Fact #89

AI CAN DIAGNOSE DISEASES BY SMELL

A I is sniffing out illness—*literally*.

Scientists have trained AI models on data from electronic noses—devices that detect chemical compounds in breath, sweat, or urine—to identify illnesses like cancer, Parkinson's, and even COVID-19. The AI can pick up on subtle scent signatures long before symptoms appear, with accuracy rivaling trained dogs. It's like giving machines a superhuman sense of smell—with life-saving potential.

Mind-Blowing
AI Fact #90

AI IS CREATING INTERACTIVE FASHION

A I is designing clothes that *respond to you.* Fashion designers are experimenting with AI-generated garments that change color, shape, or texture based on emotion, movement, or environment. In one project, a dress shifted hues based on the wearer's mood, using sensors and machine learning to analyze biometric data. It's not just style—it's *fashion that feels you back.*

Mind-Blowing AI Fact #91

AI CAN PREDICT FINANCIAL CRASHES

A I is reading the market's mood swings. Financial analysts are using AI to scan vast streams of market data, news headlines, social media sentiment, and trading behavior to detect early warning signs of economic downturns. Some models have successfully predicted sharp drops and flash crashes *hours or even days in advance.* It's like having a crystal ball—but built from code and chaos.

Mind-Blowing
AI Fact #92

AI CAN RESTORE BLURRY SECURITY FOOTAGE

A I is sharpening the past—*frame by frame.* Law enforcement agencies and video editors are using AI to enhance low-quality or blurry footage—turning pixelated messes into clearer, usable images. These models analyze patterns, facial structures, and movement to reconstruct missing details with shocking accuracy. In some cases, suspects have been identified *from video once considered useless.* It's CSI meets super-resolution.

Mind-Blowing AI Fact #93

AI CAN TRANSLATE ANIMAL GESTURES

A I is decoding what animals are *saying with movement.*

Biologists are training AI models to analyze body language in animals—like elephants, dogs, and primates—to better understand communication beyond sound. One system identified consistent "gesture phrases" in chimpanzees, suggesting a structured form of nonverbal language. It's not just barking or flapping—it's *sentences in motion.*

Mind-Blowing AI Fact #94

AI IS COMPOSING MUSIC FOR THERAPY

A I is tuning in to emotional healing.
Therapists and researchers are using AI to generate personalized music tracks designed to reduce anxiety, aid focus, or improve sleep. These systems adapt tempo, instrumentation, and harmony based on biometric feedback like heart rate or brainwaves. In clinical trials, some AI-generated music outperformed traditional playlists in calming the nervous system. It's not just background noise—it's *data-driven serenity*.

Mind-Blowing AI Fact #95

AI IS GUIDING THE BLIND IN REAL TIME

A I is becoming a second pair of eyes.

Wearable devices powered by AI are helping visually impaired individuals navigate the world by identifying objects, reading signs, and even recognizing faces—all in real time. These tools use computer vision to describe surroundings through audio prompts, giving users instant feedback about obstacles or opportunities. It's more than assistance—it's *independence, amplified.*

Mind-Blowing AI Fact #96

AI CAN PREDICT SINKHOLES BEFORE THEY FORM

A I is spotting danger *beneath our feet.*

Geologists are using AI to analyze satellite imagery, soil movement, and underground water data to predict where sinkholes might appear—*before* any visible signs. In high-risk areas, this tech has given early warnings that prevented road collapses and property damage. It's like geological intuition, powered by machine learning.

Mind-Blowing
AI Fact #97

AI IS HELPING TRAIN GUIDE DOGS

AI is shaping the next generation of service animals.

Researchers have developed AI systems that analyze hours of puppy behavior footage to identify traits linked to successful guide dog training. The AI can flag potential temperament issues or strengths earlier than human trainers can—helping save time, costs, and frustration. It's not replacing the trainer—but it's becoming *the ultimate early scout.*

Mind-Blowing
AI Fact #98

AI CAN TRACK WILDLIFE WITH DRONES

A I is watching over nature *from the sky.* Conservationists are using drones equipped with AI to track animals across vast landscapes—spotting herds, identifying species, and even counting individuals in real time. In one project, AI spotted endangered orangutans in dense jungle *faster and more accurately than human spotters.* It's like giving nature conservation a set of digital eyes with wings.

Mind-Blowing AI Fact #99

AI CAN GENERATE SYNTHETIC POPULATIONS

AI is building fake people—for real science. To test public health models, urban planning, or emergency response, researchers use AI to generate "synthetic populations"—fake citizens with realistic ages, jobs, habits, and movement patterns. These data-driven stand-ins help simulate everything from flu outbreaks to traffic jams—without risking real privacy. It's like a city full of ghosts... built for good.

Mind-Blowing AI Fact #100

AI IS HELPING DESIGN OTHER AIS

A I is now building *its own successors.*

Researchers are using AI to automate parts of neural network design, optimizing new models for speed, accuracy, and efficiency. This process, called Neural Architecture Search, allows machines to create architectures that even experts wouldn't think of. One AI-designed model beat human-engineered systems—*using less data and fewer resources.* It's not just self-improvement—it's *machine evolution.*

CONCLUSION

Congratulations! You've just explored *100 Mind-Blowing AI Facts* and taken a wild ride through some of the most surprising, strange, and inspiring things artificial intelligence is doing in our world. From robot surgeons to music-making machines, from emotion-reading algorithms to story-spinning bots, this journey has shown that AI is way more than just science fiction—it's a constantly evolving force shaping our lives in ways we're only beginning to understand.

But here's the thing about AI—it's moving faster than ever. For every fact you've read, there are countless more being written in labs, startups, studios, and classrooms all around the globe. Maybe this book sparked your curiosity, or maybe it made you do a double take at just how far technology has come. Or maybe it simply reminded you that we're living in a time where imagination and innovation are colliding in ways we never thought possible.

The truth is, the world of AI is full of mind-blowing moments—and you don't have to be a programmer or a scientist to appreciate them. All it takes is a sense of wonder, a bit of curiosity, and the question, "What's next?"

So as you close this book, don't think of it as the end. Think of it as the beginning of a future filled with stories, inventions, and breakthroughs that will continue to stretch the limits of what's possible.

Until next time, stay curious, stay inspired, and remember: the most mind-blowing AI stories... are still being written.

ACKNOWLEDGEMENTS

Creating *100 Mind-Blowing AI Facts* has been a wild, fascinating ride—one filled with curiosity, late-night research rabbit holes, and more than a few "Wait... AI can do *what now?*" moments. While my name might be on the cover, this book is the result of countless people, stories, and inspirations that helped bring it to life.

First, a huge thank you to the scientists, researchers, engineers, and storytellers who are pushing the boundaries of what artificial intelligence can do—and then sharing it with the rest of us. Your work is awe-inspiring, and this book is just a small tribute to the incredible breakthroughs you've made (and continue to make every single day).

To my friends and family—thank you for letting me ramble about brain scans, robot dogs, and deepfake drama without once asking me to switch topics. Your encouragement, patience, and enthusiasm kept this project moving forward.

To the readers: you're why this book exists. Whether you're a techie, a trivia lover, or just someone who enjoys being surprised, this book is for you. Your curiosity is what makes exploring the future so fun.

And finally, to AI itself—thank you for being so endlessly strange, brilliant, and unpredictable. You've changed the world in ways we're only beginning to understand, and I'm beyond grateful to help share just a few of those incredible moments.

Here's to curiosity, to creativity, and to a future filled with even more mind-blowing surprises.

ABOUT THE AUTHOR

Felix Grayson is a storyteller at heart, driven by an insatiable curiosity for the strange, surprising, and downright unpredictable moments that shape our world. With a passion for uncovering the wildest and most unbelievable stories in science and technology, Felix has crafted *100 Mind-Blowing AI Facts* to entertain, amaze, and spark wonder in curious minds of all ages.

When he's not diving into the latest breakthroughs or chasing down the quirkiest corners of the tech world, Felix enjoys exploring futuristic ideas, devouring science biographies, and pondering life's biggest questions over a strong cup of coffee and a good conversation. A firm believer in the magic of curiosity and the power of a great fact, Felix invites you to take this journey through the strange and mind-bending world of artificial intelligence—proving that the future is every bit as full of surprises as the past.

www.ingramcontent.com/pod-product-compliance
Lightning Source LLC
Chambersburg PA
CBHW031850200326
41597CB00012B/346